Crying in LA

Sapphic Longing in Tongues and Tears

Jasmin Benward

Tehom Center Publishing is a 501(c)3 nonprofit publishing feminist and queer authors, with a commitment to elevate BIPOC writers. Its face and voice is Rev. Dr. Angela Yarber.

Paperback ISBN: 978-1-966655-28-2

Ebook ISBN: 978-1-966655-29-9

Contents

Sunny Skies

Partly Cloudy

Chance of Rain

Showers

This book is dedicated to my muses. All of them.

Here's to bright-eyed thirty, with two suitcases and a dream because "*all of the writers are in LA.*" Thirty-four knows there's plenty of sunshine and opportunities, but that it does, *in fact*, get cold. And on occasion–it rains.

'*Probably best for the flowers.*

JASMIN BENWARD

Acknowledgments

I want to thank my holy trinity: Mugas, Ma, Lyn for imparting your love of reading and words into my DNA. To every teacher, supporter, and mentor—your pourings overflow. To Tehom Publishing Center, I am infinitely grateful.

This is a celebration of visibility and voice to greats *before, now,* and *after.*

Sunny Skies

Good Woman

Ain't nothing like a good woman
Mmm-hmm
Raised right
Loving
Kind

She feels like neo-soul
She keeps it funky
She's a 10 minute song with a hidden track
Gotta listen on to catch her
Don't sleep, and
Don't skip

Ain't nothing like a good woman
Mmm-hmm
She bright
Loves a good library
Stimulate her mind
For her, looks are secondary

She feels like a ride down pacific highway
'Can't help but stare her way
All heart-eyed and handsy
'Can't get out her face

Ain't nothing like a good woman
Mmm-hmm
She tight
Gets off on resistance

Jasmin Benward

Doesn't need the mention
Unphased by accolades
Loved by the people
Helps 'cause she wanna
A real bad mama jama

Ain't nothing like a good woman
Mmm-hmm
I like how good she is to me
Damn, is she ever good to me
I'm blessed
'Won't call it lucky

Over Coffee

Nothing brings me greater joy
Than a cup of coffee
With you and only you, my dear
At sun's rising

I get to welcome a new day
With my favorite someone
Won't you wake up already?
Didn't mean to keep you up

C'mon, have a sip with me
I love to watch you
Pretend to be coy
These here beans are from the Jamaican Blue
     Mountains
Ya Mon!

C'mon, have a sip with me
How was your week?
What's bringing you joy?
This cup is Turkish
Merhaba!

Nothing brings me greater joy
Than a cup of coffee
With you and only you, my dear
At sun's rising

Jasmin Benward

C'mon, have a sip with me
Mmm, to you in that dress
Sis, your curves are rockin'
Something 'bout Oaxacan
¡Si! ¡Si! ¡Si!

I enjoy you, my dear
I enjoy your mind
And the workings of your heart
I get to know you best over coffee

Come Close

When you come close
You feel like a Sunday
Warm cinnamon rolls rising
Don't forget the raisins!
A perfected dish
The view after a climb
Look at God's artistry
Here's looking at *you!*

When you come close
I hear tambourines
I could clap and stomp
It's obvious as hell you're my person
Choir and grape juice

When you come close
Your embrace is like a butterfly spreading its wings
Seeing a rainbow after the storm
Warmth of a fireplace in the dead of winter

When you come close
It's hot tea in a novelty mug
An ingenious loop
The perfect track
With lyrics straight from source

When you come close
Your embrace feels like cookies after cooling
Unexpected money

Jasmin Benward

High-hat drum combo
Acid jazz in the park
Make it Leimert
Extra cream and sugar
Bass guitar
No, double bass
When you come close
'Feels like all things wonderful

Black Woman

Black woman is a
Steward
Vessel
Miracle
No matter what shade on the spectrum
No matter what pronouns
No matter who she loves

Black woman is a
Sister
Sissy
Sis
Mother
Ma
Mama
Aunt
Auntie

Black woman is a
Grandmother
G-Ma
G-Mama
Meh-ma
What's a Mugas?
She's a cousin
She's a daughter

Jasmin Benward

Black woman is a person
Black woman is a human
And for all the women who should be here
But aren't
Say her name

Shuffle

Hold on
Take time to fall in love
Don't get lost in the shuffle

I'm so into you
Your beady little eyes
Will you break me off a little something?
Or
Is it too soon?

Don't mind my nonsense
Love drunk off your essence
'Can't play it cool

Would you believe me
If I told you
This poem came from a few liked songs on shuffle

Creator

God herself
Dropped you in cocoa powder
Added gold for shimmer
Let you dry in the sun
All in a day's work

She brushed little star twinkles for glisten
In your perfect almond eyes
Probably before her lunch break

And before day's end
She put on her hard hat
Goggles and a patterned smock
Chiseled your body

She dyed your hair with cloves
After this she calls it one
She doesn't rush a masterpiece
Tomorrow's another day

90s Vixen

You a little
Off-drum pattern
Quirky-ass dance, you
Shimmy something different
I'm a fan
I like it
'Reminds me of a 90s vixen

I see you with your little
Capri pants, and
Crop top
Platform shoes and such
I'm a fan
I like it
'Reminds me of a 90s vixen

You *so fine* with your little
Butterfly clips and flat twists
Hoop earrings
Brown lip liner
I'm a fan
I like it
'Reminds me of a 90s vixen

Will you be my personal Nia?

Switch

I know in the streets you like oversized clothes
Loafers when you dress up, but–
I *also* know
A woman lies beneath
I love when we're alone
I *get* to see your curves

It does something to me when your
Locs glide through my fingers
I get *so excited*
Pulling down your boxers to–
Reveal hip-dips
I get *so* ecstatic
Reveling in full lips
Chunky and supple
I want them everywhere and then some

Don't get me started on your shoulders and your
    breasts
May I cup them, *suck them?*
Press them up against my chest?

Turn the lights off
I don't need everyone on Crenshaw
Seeing what's for me

Date Night

You're a museum
And the art contents inside
You're beautiful
Wow!
Wow!
Wowie!
You're a rare collection
Meant for observation and admiration

Your dimensions pull me in
Your colors and your textures
Deep indigos and magentas, mauves and the like

I look closely to see
Just what you're made of
I'm enamored at the crafts-woman-ship
The creator did her big one
Her talent speaks across space and time
Her creativity's unmatched

You're a museum
And the art contents inside
You're stunning
Ooh!
Ooh!
Ooh-ie!
Such the wonder
You're a rare collection
Meant for observation and admiration

God Is A Woman

Coochie, coochie, coochie
Pocketbook, pocketbook
Vagina
Pussy

Does that make you uncomfortable?
Magnificent!

Coochie, coochie, coochie
Pocketbook, pocketbook
Vagina
Pussy

Strong
Fruit bearing
And only if she/they want to
Our bodies
Our choice

'Meant for praise and worship, and that's
At the minimum

Vulva
Labia
Folds
Lips

Vulva
Labia
Folds
Lips

Kissy, kissy, kissy
God is a woman

Nasty

You *so* nasty!
Why not be?
Do you like it?
How does it feel?
Is *this* what you need?

I'm *real* nasty
I'm the type to talk you through it
We just may laugh a bit in the act
Ain't nothing to it!
We do what we want!

I want you–
Squealing
Scraping
Singing
Slobbing
And everything in between

I'll make sure it's
Satisfying
Scintillating
Savagery
'Cause I'm a freak
And that's what freaks do

Yeah, I'm real nasty
Don't tell my mother

Are you high yet?
To the moon yet?
Some unknown galaxy?

Christen me in your sweat
I could use the cooling

You *so* nasty!
All you think about is–
I know
Ready for round three?

'Gon flip yourself around
Turn over for me

I want you–
Screaming
Slippery
Shouting
Sobbing
And everything in between

Yeah, I'm real nasty
Don't tell my mother

Production

I do very well at
Holding my tongue
I've been waiting
To say something
Out of pocket

Sometimes I wonder
If we were to paint a picture together
Sonically
If we were to fiddle with choices
What would they be?

I'd want snaps for sure
Lots of bass
And 808s
Hella strings and pluckin'
Put the hats back in

Probably a choir
Whirls and keys
Lil' vocalese maybe
Definitely tambourines

I'd try not to self-edit
I'd try everything
To see what sticks and what lands

Crazy Feelings

Your presence is–
Magnificent
I'm out of body
I've got
Crazy feelings

There's an
Absence of pride
When it comes to you
It's whatever

I'd kiss your hands and feet
You can get it all from me
Tell me *what's wrong*
Let me fix it

There's an
Absence of pride
When it comes to you
It's whatever

I'd do anything for you
Pick you up from LAX
Find a park after six in K-Town
It's whatever for you
These must be
Crazy feelings

Send It On

Send me
Somebody's Black-Brown daughter to love and
    love me
I want to breathe her air

Send me
Somebody's Black-Brown daughter to love and
    love me
I'd live for her stare

Send me
Somebody's Black-Brown daughter to love and
    love me
I crave a romance
Something like a *Love Jones*
Or
90s R&B

Send me
Somebody's Black-Brown daughter to love and
    love me
I'll write her poems just like these
'Make her my muse

Send her on
Send her on
Send her on

'Wouldn't be mad at an overnight delivery

You Ain't Shy

You *ain't* shy
And *I know*
That *you know*
That *I know*
That you know
That
I know
So
Why lie?
Whatever you wish for is safe with me

Tell me what you want me to do

Cinematic

Wanna be in love *so good* it feels
Cinematic
Maybe I'd break out into song
Like a musical
Bet it'd be hella fun
Full of action and adventure

We could have dance numbers
And battle in the kitchen
Anyone within eyesight
Would know that it's a romance
Anytime that we're together

We could get *real* crafty
And eat each other whole

Wanna be in love *so good* it feels
Cinematic
I get feels enough to skittle in the ally
Down cobblestone
With peppery steps and a big, fat smile
With assurance that you're mine

You're so darn lovely
You bring out my best takes

Wanna be in love *so good* it feels
Cinematic

My very own happily ever after
Hold the Hollywood divorce

I Want You

I want you like the Black collective
Group economics, and no spend days
I want you like I want greatness
I want you like legacy
I want you like reparations

I want you like no limits
I want you like no ceiling over me
I want you like a blessing

I want you like knowledge
I want you like wealth pouring over me
I want you like rain showering crops in my garden

I want you now
Don't you know?
You *should* know

I want you like a push from my higher self
I want you, like
For *really* real

Perception

Where others see nappy texture
I see hydrangeas growing from your roots
But that's cause I'm a poet

Where others see tar
I see deep night wrapping your flesh and bones
But that's cause I'm a poet

Where others see a wide nose
I see an expansive field for all my kissing
But that's cause I'm a poet

Perception is a funny thing

Sweet Thang

You're my little honey comb
Red velvet cheesecake

Oh, sweet thang!

You're my little peanut butter brittle
Or are you praline?

Oh, sweet thang you are!

You're my little concha
More like flan

Oh, sweet thang!

You're my little chocolate chip cookie
Minus the chips
It ain't the same as a plain sugar
Trust me on this one

Oh, sweet thang!

I know my way around a bakery
You belong in a display case
I could marvel at you all day, day
'Cause you're my little sweet thang

Oh, sweet thang!

You so fine, you blow my mind
Pretty, pretty sweet thang

Oh, sweet thang!

Think about you all the time
Lovely, little sweet thang

Extraordinary

You're something like a phenomenon
Your kiss ignites a fire inside of me
I get chills to the touch
You've got my permission
To have me forever, and–
That wouldn't be enough
You so extraordinary

You're something like a phenomenon
I imagine the thrill of you inside of me
You're so extraordinary
Out of this world, sista
Shit, damn, motherfucker
Sailor mouth when I'm lovin' you
Never had it like *this* before

You're something like a phenomenon
You've got my permission
To pull *all* my levers, and–
It's never too much

You so extraordinary

Black Love Scene

When the lights go down
We retire to bed
And
Orchestrate our own little Black love scene
It's
Opulent
Luxurious, and
Radiant

When the lights go down
We retire to bed
And
Orchestrate our own little Black love scene
It's
Electric
Pulsing
Panting, and
Full of longing

We know that it's a mean, cruel world outside
For people like us
Who love like we do
Inside we've built a home for each other

When the lights go down
We retire to bed
And
Orchestrate our own little Black love scene

Jasmin Benward

It's
Safe
Secure, and–
Most importantly it's
Sure

Inner Thoughts Come Spring

God, I *love* the springtime
I've beat the winter blues
I'm alright
In the thick of the super bloom

God, I *love* the springtime
I'm better
I get to see your ass sitting pretty in a sundress
Sun percolating all your melanin
Bless me
I smile your way casually
We sit underneath an oak tree
Truth is
I'm burning up
My inner speak is loud

God, I can hardly
Is that a fresh twist out?
I high-key wanna ruin it
What am I thinking about?
Just you
Did you see her cool ass fade 'cross the lawn?

God, I *love* the springtime
It's made for stepping out
You look fly as fuck
You a bad-ass jawn
You look even better all laid out on this here blanket

Jasmin Benward

Your head nested in my lap
'Probably better on top of me
I want *you* to be my snack
Fuck
This
Charcuterie

God, I *love* the springtime
Let's get outta here
Yes, I'll take your picture first
By the cherry blossoms
'Just might pluck you a rose
But don't tell nobody

God, I *love* the springtime
Is that an anklet?
You know I like shiny things
Toe ring, too?
Girl, you are sending me
Lord, have mercy
I can't take it!

God, I *love* the springtime
I should feed you
It's only right
Should *I* choose?
Or do you know what you want?

We could get pizza
Craving doubles
They don't have that here

Wouldn't mind sushi
I'll eat out of your hands

God, I *love* the springtime
It's even better
With you

Process

I'm no beginner
I haven't gotten complaints to date
But I must learn your body
'Part of my process
You're a new place
That I've never been before

I'll have to learn
When and where to accelerate
Which parts of you are tender
And when I do
Heaven help you
I'll deliver

My sentiment's enduring
Physical stamina to match
If only you'll sing to me
I can get you there quicker

I'll listen for which rhythm
Play until I find your key
I won't deny that I live for
The sound of my excellence
'Bet I can get you higher

It's
Part of my process
You're a new place
That I've never been before

This is
Enchanted exploration
Creative inquiry

And we could go all night
All night
All night
We could go all night
All night

It's
Part of my process
Standard procedure
You're a new place
That I've never been before

And we could get it on
'Til the morning
Morning
Morning
I want you happily yawning at work

Death By Chocolate

Turns out you're my playground
Honey, I *love* to play
You're moisturized real good for me
Softened in butter cream shea
Slick coconut oil drips down your round brown
　　bottom
I can't keep from melting

Turns out you're my playground
Honey, I *love* to play
Your swollen mounds are
Made for my mouth
And if I don't fall out
From heat exhaustion
It'll be death by chocolate

Night Shift

If I was hired
I'd work *the hell* out of you
Treat it like a job

I'd clock in
And punch out
I'd even keep a log
I'd beg for overtime

Did you know?
The average human skin cell
Is about 30 micrometers in diameter
10,000 hours is a *long time*
Mastery's my motivation
It's all in repetition—*no?*
Two, three, six times just won't cut it

'Cause if *I* was hired
I'd work *the hell* out of you
Treat it like a job

Report
Again and again and again
Again and again and again
Again and again some more

Questions

Once at nine o'clock
Again at midnight
Wake you up at dawn

I've got questions

Can you keep up?
How much can you take?
Is it good to you?
Should I beg for it?
May I please have more?

You've made a real fiend
Out of me

I've got questions

Are you up?
I'm not tired
How do you like it?
Is it mine?

You've made such the fiend
Out of me

Kissy-Kissy

There's nothing better than to
Make out with a pretty lady, who
Knows how to kiss

Sure, it's part chemistry, but
Kisses tell you everything you need to know
Trust me
I've had lots of practice

It shouldn't be *too* fast
But have some pressure
Not *too, too* slow
Maybe just a little tongue
It should feel warm and electric

I've been known to see colors
Blame it on the synesthesia
I know a good kiss when I feel it
Chills should shoot up and down your spine, and
Make your coochie do backflips and curl
I'm dramaful, but
This is no exaggeration
If you don't feel anything
She's not your girl

Slow Dance

I wanna slow dance with you
At the rent party
We pretend to be motown mamas
We sway *too* close and grind
I look into your eyes
Trap you with my gaze

Alls I gotta do is
Approach the nape of your neck and *breathe*
I want you crazy for me
Like I am you

I wanna slow dance *real grown* with you
Whine at the bashment
The lights are low, and
The reggae's thumpin'
That makes two of us

Alls I gotta do is
Approach the nape of your neck and *breathe*
I want you crazy for me
Like I am you

I wanna groove with you
Faster at the cook-out
Two-step and back up *my stuff*
Line dance and such
'Try not to step on your toes

I'm in love with you
'Wonder if you know
Heart's beating *hella* fast
Breathing *hella* fast
Waiting to exhale

I want you *crazy* for me
Like I am you

I'm in love with you
'Wonder if you know

Passport

I wonder 'round on this silly little passport
Feeling like an avatar with play money
Until I see—
Shanty towns and cardboard houses
How fortunate am I to have *agency*
This radicalizes me
I *do* have privilege
How I love to travel the world

I wonder 'round on this silly little passport
Feeling like an avatar with play money
Until I see—
Lovers kiss through cracked glass, and
This radicalizes me
Now I love to travel the world

How lucky am I to have autonomy?
How blessed am I to have my eyes to see?
How wonderful to have experiences
Hawthorne ain't done nothing to me, but
The world's a big, big place

The Morning After

I raise the blackout curtains
Letting the light creep in
Taking inventory as you stand at attention
Committing your every curve to memory
With your morning stretch

Every freckle, scar, and mole
I get cool without your body heat
Now that we're not in bed
I should invest in heated floors
A weighted blanket, for
When you can't make it

I'm hoping you'll return and sooner than later
To keep me warm again

Sex Magic

We've got a tantric practice
My legs are straddled
Over your waist
Yours over mine
Heart-to-heart
We charge each other up
The truth lies in the eyes

Our bodies are interlaced
I softly kiss your neck and face
Whispering affirmations in your ears
I'm happy to be in this moment
Sharing sacred space with you

I'm intrigued by your mind
The goodness that is, *you*
And your lips when they say nothing at all
When they talk about anything
Specifically, your passions
All the things that drive your ambition
I listen, and intently
'Put my hand over your heart
It beats with a familiar bass
Connection is critical

I *love* when we make magic
Couch
Room

Kitchen
Shower
On the floor—magic

Sub

I close my lids
For something a little different
Not keen on vanilla right now

We're in a dark room
Anonymous figures linger
Hover left and right in a cadence
To see you standing firm in your power

My arms are outstretched
Across a wooden X
You're just beyond my shoulder
There's a menacing red flicker in your eyes
I know that you've got demons
They're out to play tonight

What will it be *this time?*
Might I be forced to clean you up?
The figures onlook
At the spectacle we've made

My temperature's rising
A band cuts into my wrist
Indicating no inhibition
I've arrived for full play

It's damp in this chamber
I hear the grind of your chains drip from your body
And screech beyond the floor

You smack my ass
I'm a willful champion
Vibrations of Edm music pulses
I hear anonymous groans

You spit for me to swallow
Open, you demand
I surrender
Do as I'm told
You crave my limits
My capacity unknown
My tolerance for you knows no bounds

I feel welts rising
With every *swish, swish* of your whip
I anticipate more
You have no mercy for me

After I'm crawling at your feet
You kneel down
Squish my chin
And slap me

My fishnets *tear*
My panties *moisten*
My center *hums*
The strobe lights are glaring

I have no choice but surrender
I'm strapped in the darkness
You won't release my leash
You step on my back

Jasmin Benward

I lick your hands feverishly–in worship

I whimper
The bass weighing on my pulse
I call you daddy
'Cause it turns you on
Am I your perfect little sub?

Just as the figures close in, I
Explode

I have such the vivid imagination
It's just you and me here
In our bedroom
Doing what we do
Perks of an unhinged writer

Partly Cloudy

Moment In Time

We wiggle at the cafe
While groovy indie rock plays
Producing new insiders, just as
Silly as ever

Do you like my new bowl cut?
Should I try a shag next?
What about a fade?
'Think I could pull it off?

I shouldn't keep your opinions of me *too close*
Not like the oversized olive-green sweater I wear
This will all just be the past some day

We order matching earl-grey lavender lattes
We get frothy-milky hearts
With red snapdragon flowers for color

I should lock arms with you just a bit closer
This will all just be a memory some day

Something 'bout a moment in time
Something 'bout naivete
It fuels me
'Gives me hope
A little optimism that you'll be mine for a lifetime
Not just in this moment

Hopeless Romantic

I envision things like
Soft kissing your shoulders, *no*
Your clavicles, *that's sexier*
While you put your makeup on
A hopeless-ass romantic

I imagine shit like
Eating a noodle from opposite ends
Of course you are the lady
I'm the tramp
A goofy-ass romantic

I'd pay to
Make sweet love to you
With a harp playing in the next room, *or*
Maybe a sitar
While I'm
All
Up
In
Your
Guts, girl
A freaked-out romantic

I dream of exhausting possibilities to engage
        with you
'Keep you happy
And on your toes
A hoping-ass romantic

Anchor

We've got turbulence in waters once calm
Really?
How did this transpire?
Are we—
Are we gonna get better?
I need to know now

We've sailed so far from shore
I couldn't be further out
Inland ain't nowhere in sight
It's not about knowing how to swim at this point

Really
Are we—
Are we gonna get better?
I need to know
Now
Should I anchor myself?
Before we're lost for sure

Ain't Got It

I'm obedient
I answer to the woman below
She tells me what I need to know
And if she tells me *no*
You just *ain't* got it

I'm choosy, and
You can't be my candy
If you ain't got the right stuff
I like mine rough around the edges
And real sweet on me

If she ain't hard about you
Hip-hoppin'
Beatboxing–
Next!
No lordy!
You can't be my shorty
I don't like my Mister Softee cone sprinkle-free

Deadass

If she don't two-step and shuffle like
Second line
In the summertime of New Orleans
No, baae
You can't be my ol' lady
Ya pralines 'gon need some 'mo sugar

Make groceries

You not 'gon
Worry
Stress
Underwhelm me
Have me pissed off on the 405
Sitting in traffic
Mad 'cause I gotta come home to you
No ma'am

Let's save ourselves the trouble
Been really nice to know you, but–

It's
All-in or alone for me
I'm obedient
I answer to the woman below
She tells me what I need to know
And if she tells me *no*
You just *ain't* got it

I hope that I don't make you feel
Like leftovers
Nestled in the back of the fridge
Forgotten and expired, but
You just *ain't* got it
She told me *no*

I've been in your shoes
The girl that chases

Jasmin Benward

Is never chosen
Last to be picked
I know it hurts, but
She told me *no, so*
I ain't got it for ya

Voyeur

I hate social media
There's an omnipresence
I can't get away from
Digital trail
There's no such thing as being over when you're
Done
Somebody's steady watching

No love letters
No apologies
No bended knees
Just assumptions of how *I'm living*
And what *I* got going on, or
What I don't
Based on what you see

Well, my number hasn't changed
Nor my email
Everything's the same
You would know if you used them
'Should have blocked your ass
But there's something about hope

You wouldn't know my darkness
Much remains unknown
Words can be knives
Is this why you chose the quiet?
Silence is a language all its own

Jasmin Benward

So you watch me
No words
You think you know me
You don't
You're just a voyeur
Monitoring spirit
Or whatever they call 'em

Imagination

Will I forever wonder
Where your hands would go first
Will I forever wonder
If they're
Perky
Supple
Drooping
Big or small

Will I forever wonder
If she's
Thin
Fat
Puffy

Will I forever wonder?

'Guess I'll lean on my imagination

Can You Feel It?

When I look at *you*
Warmth sits inside me

When I look at *us*
I see dreams fulfilled

We're bigger than where we come from
We hold tight to the wisdom of the ones who came
    before us
We're advancing our lineages
Can you feel it?

We've taken the baton and carried on
We're–
Badder, bolder, stronger
Than our mama's-mama's-mama
Standing on shoulders
Breaking generational curses
Can you feel it?

We knew that we were made for better
So we're doing it together
Our love is radical *you and me*
Being free unapologetically, and
Out loud
Can you feel it?

I meditate on you and with you

I wish you well when I kiss you
I pray for you while you sleep
Can you feel it?

Chance of Rain

Walking Shoes

Something tells me, I
Should keep my walking shoes nearby
I'm Baldwin overlooked
'Busted up and all

'Probably intuition
I feel that you're different
If you change your mind about us
I should be the first to know, no?

'Guess I'll tie up my walking shoes
Threads hanging and laces loose
Grab my things and get gone
Up the stairs to nowhere

I'm going
You don't have to fuss me out
I'm going
And you bet not touch my stuff!
I'm going

I don't want to work it out
I don't want to figure it out
This isn't what I pictured

I won't cry here
But I'm all torn up, that
You don't want me no more
You don't want me no more

Jasmin Benward

I won't cry here
You can't have that benefit
You treat me like anybody off the street
'Wonder what I tried so hard for

I won't cry here
But I'm all torn up, that
You don't want me no more
You don't want me no more

Forbidden Fruit

Why you gotta be such a sight for sore eyes?
Why do you elicit cravings on my tongue?
I salivate upon you nearing
Internal slithers occur
Your presence demands my attention
Rousing my inner snake

I'll go too far with it
To experience you
I'll exercise my free will, and—
Let my demons win

I'd say it's worth the karma
To feel our mouths interlaced, in
Dishonorable indulgence
A gluttony of flesh

I'd do it
Despite the consequences
I need it
You know it, too
'Bet you get off on the tease
It's prolly edging for you

I just need *one time*
My hands won't be mine
I'll know no self-restraint
I've been longing for *too long*
I'll all but bite you and break skin

Jasmin Benward

I'll go *too far* with it
To experience you
I'll exercise my free will, and–
Let my demons win
You make me uncomfortably feral
More than anyone

You're forbidden fruit
I'd devour every bit of you
Eat you whole
With juices dripping down my chin
Down to seed and core

I'd act like I've never had it
I'd act a damn fool

Why you gotta be such a sight for sore eyes?
Why do you elicit cravings on my tongue?

Stupid

It was *stupid*
I believed
That showing up for you could mean something
We are now
On the other side
Of adoration and loving
Doubt you'll like the new me
One of a jaded, bitter, annoyed woman

I was *stupid*
I saw a unit
I saw mutual aid
I saw collaboration
Before the fires
I saw home-schooling
Before the dismantling whispers
Foresight is stupid
I sound crazy, don't I?

We are now
On the other side
Of adoration and loving
Doubt you'll like the new me
One of a jaded, bitter, annoyed woman

I saw a village
I saw harmony
I saw the bed of our own

Jasmin Benward

I saw you smiling
I saw your privacy
I would have been discreet
Visions are stupid
I sound delusional, don't I?

Love and Logic

Love and logic
Logic and love
Two concepts that don't go together
Not one bit, *no*
Not at all

Passenger's Side

I can't begin to recollect
How many images I've captured
In pure resentment
Staring out the passenger's side
I don't want to look at you
You've hurt my feelings and you know it, don't you?
Yeah, you do

You insult my intelligence
You think that I don't notice
How you treat me versus everyone else
I swear this is the *very last time*
That *I* get tolerated
'Tired of the lovers-to-enemies-trope thing, that I
Seem to have going on

Arm's out the window
I want to feel *something*
I feel alone in your presence
Should've just stayed my ass home
Rather, I should just move out, and
Go it alone
Hate that I've overstayed far too many welcomes

Street signs
Palm trees
Unhoused
The beach

Plazas
Pedestrians
Bus stops
All looking back at me, like
Why don't you do something?

Onward

I'll be right here where you left me
Stay where you are
You're *so sorry*
Not *actually* sorry
I deserve more

I see no need to go back
I'm a-going onward
I'll be right here where you left me

You can stay where you at
You're *so sorry, not sorry*
I see no need to go back
I'm a-going onward

I'll be right here where you left me
You can stay where you at
You're *so* sorry, *not* sorry
I see no need to go back
I'm a-going onward

I don't want my mail
I don't care about the sock I left behind
Throw it all away
I don't want to hear from you
'Wish I could erase you from my life

On Stage

I'll never forget
The warm up
Standing in an oval
Doing exercises
Getting ready for the show

You had such the glow
You deserved to be *on stage*
Without hidden conditions

From you
I learned
The delicate intimacies
Of creative play
It's been excruciating
Living with release
I never really wanted

Your energy was contagious
I couldn't be told *no,* but
Actually
Yes, and
You excited me
Like I've never felt before

From you
I learned
The delicate intimacies
Of creative play

Jasmin Benward

It's been quite the mind-fuck
Living with release
I never really wanted

It meant everything to me to see you shine the way
    you did
And do
Whether or not I'm in your picture

I watched on in wonder
You had such the glow
And I'll never forget those silly little exercises

Life is a stage

You Ain't No Friend

Damn, girl
Again?
A rain check again?
You ain't no friend
You like the access

Damn, girl
Again?
Withholding again?
Hollywood is getting to you
You ain't no friend
It's all strategy

Damn, sis
Damn
You watched me struggling
Laughed, instead of leaning in
You ain't no friend

Damn, sis
Damn
I let you in
Let you use my shit
Told you all my business
Here we go again
'Feels like I'm begging
You make things harder for me, and *unnecessarily*
Yo, like, I can't

Jasmin Benward

It's on me, truly
I'll do a better job next time of
Deciphering
Colleague to associate to nothing
'Can't just be calling any-'ol-body
A friend

Scorched

Something 'bout this water to coffee ratio ain't right
That's what happens when you use instant
Now, I'm french-pressed and bitter
No amount of cream and sugar can remedy this

I'm green tea steeped well over time
I've missed the mark
Ain't worth a damn
This ain't about no damn tea

Go on, it won't hurt nothing
Go on, have a drink
Fuck!
'Scorched my tongue
Now I can't taste anything
Not without the reminder

I'm 'gon learn about impulse
I'm 'gon learn how to take my time
I'm 'gon learn discernment
Or it will be the death of me

Outdoors for a little too long
Exposed with no protection
I've missed the mark
Ain't worth a damn
This ain't about sunscreen

Jasmin Benward

I'm 'gon learn about impulse
I'm 'gon learn how to take my time
I'm 'gon learn intentionality
Or it will be the death of me

Showers

Montage

I've got
Cycle blues, with
Crimson gut-punches
Feels like kung-fu drop-kicks-to-my-lower-back
Those type-a-lows
Craving something Thai or deeply fried
Down bad
And I'm
Feeling dreadful, *horrible even*
Then it all dawned on me
This is more than me being in my feelings
This ain't about the cramps

This is split screen montage
When you go your way and I go mine
This is separation
This is moving on, but
Hardly fine

This is split screen montage
I sit on the couch without a heating pad and no
    snacks
No shoulder to lean on, with
Far too many chocolates and no meal
Just a-heaving and a-crying
With the score of a sad song

This is split screen montage
You celebrate an anniversary

Jasmin Benward

The day of my birthday
I get the misfortune of
Thinking of you on my birthday
Alone at the bar
And I don't even drink no more
I'd drown in so-called harmless grapefruit martinis
Just a-down and out about cha

Fragments

Oh, what do *I* know?
What remains in
Fiber forming disrupted
Organic from synthetic
Who am *I* to tell?

I tell you what–
Fragments
Sediment of something solid
Fallen petals from a rose
Leaving stem and thorns in my hands
'Held too tight
'Should've let go

Stuck with hurt feelings
Oh, I know she loves that

Bruised-brown pride
Speckles-on-speckles
Chocolate chip on my shoulder
'Makings of *warm, gooey, banana bread,* but
Fuck!
Ain't no baking soda!
Nevermind it

I remember everything
My mind's database stored pictures of you smiling
I pull them from time-to-time

Jasmin Benward

I remember everything
I know your favorite color
Mustard, myer, canary–
Whatever it's called
You're *everywhere* to me
Find you
Everywhere I go
You're *all* over LA
Feel you in Mexico

I craved a constant
Croissants and early coffees
Morning pages
You, you, you, you, you
A trap kick-drum

I waited another year after you told me *no*
I waited another half year after you told me you
        won't
I've never clung to the word won't
So
Hard
Before
It's not like *shouldn't* or *can't*
It's the *no* of choice

It hurt to let someone else touch me
I couldn't feel anything
Even when I tried
Why didn't I feel anything?

Because it wasn't you

You sure did have a hold on me
You sure *do* have a hold on me
No, no, no, no, no

I wished for my hands on your walnut mommy
    tummy
I bet there was honey in your mouth
I long for the gaze of your hazy eyes
That seemingly called me by my name
Why did I stare your way too long?
Because–
I saw oceans

I would have taught you to swim
I'd never let anything happen to you
Not under my watch
You were my treasure
'Treat you like precious cargo

I'm not one for diamonds
I *did* pray that God would give me you
You felt like Christmas, and
I said it 'cause I meant it
'Never had a reason to lie
Never meant to cause you harm
'Could have done it all better
If I had a tape I would rewind, and
Re-record

'Probably for the best I didn't get my way
I probably woulda quit all my other vices
And made fucking you a habit

Jasmin Benward

Never-ever have a roster, and
Probably never ever want another

I was *well on my way* to love
Can you blame me?

Are you not embarrassed?
I ask self
Do you have no chill?
Who is there to put on for?
I answer
Who am *I* to be bashful?
It doesn't matter anymore
You don't want me–
At least not anymore
It's not happening, Jasmin
What are all the poems for?

'Held *too-damn-tight*
Should've let go
You are hard to quit
But eventually I will
I am
There's *progress*
Coming off you every day with the absence
No negative space in the image
I don't fit in the family photos
'Thought my shit was fool proof
Looking extra goof-y

Wanna know something?

All of my favorite poems that turn out the way that I
    want them to
Are about you
Ain't that nothing?!

Languages Of Love

Acts of service
Someone making life easier for me
Can you imagine?

Physical touch
Someone to hold me and give me what I need
Someone with affections
Who can keep up!
Can you imagine?

I'm not big on gifts
But shit
I like flowers just because it's Tuesday
Thoughtful little somethings every once in awhile
'Be nice
Can you imagine?

Words of affirmation
Now we're talking baby!
I work *too damn hard* to not get a good word
Encouragement helps wonders
Can you imagine?

Quality time is what captures me most
'Just wanna be up under you
Doing everything and nothing
Could be nice
Can you imagine?

Not For Me

My shell repels the parts of you
That you believe that I can't see
You remind me of old versions
I no longer want to be

I know you don't love yourself
I know you look to your past as reverence
Instead of acting in the now
I know what you don't–*preparedness speaks*

As harsh is this may sound
It comes from a good place
Don't wait until you've met your match
To get it all together
Train in waiting
That type of thing
Do what you must to heal and get better

I'm an old bitch
I don't want a project
Just to get my ideal ever after

It's a feeling that I get
It's my intuition
That says you're just not ready for me

Good Grief

Would you court yourself?
Why, yes!
I believe I would

Ego aside
I've yet to meet another me

She should be–
Cultured
Whimsical
Well-traveled
A music savant
A cooking master
With an expansive palette
God-fearing
Good-weird
Fun-loving
A full-on freak

Not to toot my own horn or anything
But I could use a little
Good grief

Selfish Black Futurism

In another multiverse
You could teleport
And split yourself across timelines
I am not a distraction
I am not

In this world
Other people's opinions don't exist
Taking more than one lover isn't taboo
In this world I am chosen

There aren't flying cars, but
Maybe green cities
Everything's walkable
It's hot when it's supposed to be hot
It's cold when it's supposed to be cold
Living is abundant
No one wants for anything
I can afford LA rent
Dare I say a mortgage?

We have freshly-pressed juices over color swatches
Probably beet or orange
You consult on my new reading nook
I choose a moody hunter green for my library
We break for Indian
I get butter chicken
You have vegetable biryani
You ask for a *little sip*, then proceed to

Jasmin Benward

Drink up all my lassi

I put on some obscure vinyl
Nothing too distracting
Dug it at the thrift, as
I read to you from a book on my coffee table
It's probably the feng shui one
Sandal-rose incense burns and smokes
Your onyx legs stretch across my sectional
Your chipped toes are in my lap
When you look away I tickle you, and
Tease *that's what you get*

Kind of sucks
No, it actually sucks
Never getting to explore this side of who you are
This is just a single vignette of how I see you
In selfish Black futurism

False Victory

'Thought we had something special
Big, big, bait and switch
False victory
I don't belong to you
You don't belong to me
I hate that I hang on to your every word like this
I miss you
Not everyday now, but most
Some
It's dwindling
I don't like it

Something 'bout your sleepy eyes
Intense, yet over everything
'You still smoking like a chimney?
Your locs are budding beautifully
This whole distant witness thing is no fun for
        me, but
I'm not breaking no-contact

I may have overstayed my welcome
I may have missed the initial message
Blame it on the 'tism
Social cues be eating my ass up
But by now I've got the hint
I don't think I have another false victory within me
Not after you

Shit damn-near took me out

Stagnant Possibilities

My imagination gets me into trouble, I saw
Scuba diving in Cuba
I held your hand under the sea
We got massages in Sayulita
I think too vividly, I saw

London and Amsterdam
Sparking up in cafes
Cheersing ales in pubs
I saw too much

I grieve stagnant possibilities

My mind captured dirty whispers at the dining table
Dimly lit
Full of giggles
Think we were in Brooklyn
Neither here nor there

I'm stuck with a bill of stagnant possibilities
Everything and nothing
Wanted to bend you over balconies
All over the world, in
Boutique hotels with
White linens
Take your arm at crosswalks, and
Call you my girl
I mourn the days when you checked for me

I grieve the stagnant possibilities
A love bottlenecked on I-10

Type Shit

You had me wide
Wiiiiiiiideeeeeeee
Wide the fuck open
'Had my petals just a-going
Something like a lotus
Real, real wide

I think the problem is
I bloomed especially for you
And everyone could tell
Like everyone
I tried to hide it

You had me wide
Wiiiiiiiideeeeeeee
Wide the fuck open
Feeling like a fairy
Your enchanting ass
Witchcraft and wizardry
Wide, real wide
Had me swirling
Circles at the disco
Feeling like a queen

Too outwardly sensual
I'm sure that was my problem
Quiet as it's kept

Too damn wide
Wiiiiiiiideeeeeeee
With my chest out, and
My heart on my sleeve

Type shit to work if it can work
A disaster when it don't, but
Magnetism speaks

Seeing Green

She's got green eyes
It's *so* obvious
Everybody sees it
Wherever we go

I think it's envy
'Would say she's jealous
Oh baby, be lucky she got to you first
I'd be the worst about you

Her eyes are grass in the spring
A four-leaf clover
Toad on a lily
Cucumber salad

She's a flower-stem shorty
She hates me
I'm sure

I can't help that this here is organic
I can't help that it's natural

Don't fault me, but
I must ask
Are you happy?
'Cause if not say word

Pudding And Worms

Oh, you're alive!
You're *not* dead?
Just dead to me
You're a little dirt-cup-snack on Halloween
Chocolate pudding, worms, and cookies
I was digging you for nothing

Signs

The further I get into this love game
I've arrived at an understanding
Some call it red flags
When you've been decentered
When there's no more love
When the well's run dry
There will be–*signs*

'Enough to make you wonder
If there was any care for you at all

This is just my experience, but
Your "so-called" lover
Will claim to be private
You won't be loved out loud
Subtle as they seem there will be–*signs*
A whole lot of nit-picking

And when you notice
Don't lead with your heart
Get it out your mind
Run expeditiously
They'll fool you well
Feed on your naivete

You'll wonder if there was any care at all
No rules in *love and war*
They won't make concessions
There will be no grace

They'll call you out your name
And claim your over sensitivity
They'll threaten accountability, and
'Tell you you should *go*
With very little notice

This is just my experience, but
Your *so-called* lover will be a professional, at
Light dimming
Always playing devil's advocate
Against your best interest
Highly competitive
Mind-blowingly selfish

That's not how you treat someone you love

This is just my experience, but
Your *so-called* lover will maximize your doubts
Hike up your insecurities
Give you anxiety
Laugh and play it off
Pose themselves as shelter
When they don't mean you better
Not-so-secret malice
And harm
They'll be slow to complement for fear you get them
    often
There will be signs
Be cautious not to miss them

I myself don't have the wherewithal for another
    narcissist

117

Jasmin Benward

And when you notice
Don't lead with your heart
Get it out your mind
Run expeditiously
They'll fool you well
Feed on your naivete
They *love* a good ego stroke
They need excess attention
You'll pour and pour and pour and pour
Never get a mention
I hope that you're listening

There will be signs

One Word

One word
Sorry
It's as if you don't know it
Like poison on your tongue
Two syllables to spit out
Pff! Pff! Pff!

One word
Sorry
Some mantra you've rebuked and sworn off
It's not in your vocabulary
You don't know it

One word
Sorry
Like a stranger
That you see and choose to cross the street instead
To walk on the other side
Not even *I apologize*

Is it vanity?
You know her well
Was I just *something to do?*
You've chosen to ghost me
I know that you surveil me–quietly
Why don't you ever just say it
I'm sorry

Julia Roberts

I'm in love with you, and
Someone else has your heart
It's pragmatic
Responsible
What you 'ought to do
It's virtuous
Expected
Acceptable
Last one in
First one out
I'm rotting in the friend-zone
But we're not really friends, are we?

Someone's chasing me, but
I don't want her
I want you
It's all a vicious cycle
A complicated matter
Round and round in loops we go
Getting so far nowhere

I could submit, yield, surrender
Mama didn't raise a quitter
I want to change your mind

I want to win your heart
I should be your selection
We're so good together
We laugh about anything

A smile never leaves my face
Or do you not remember?

I desire you beyond the pages
My eyes dilated
That's not something that you make up
What about the art?
How am I supposed to write?
I'll put out garbage without a muse

She Hate Me

There's absolutely nothing worse
Than ill-meaning energy in your personal orbit
An opp guised as a partner
Can y'all believe I had her hating-ass-hands in my
    hair?
She touched my crown with sinister delight
She hated me
Was rough with my edges
And kept me on edge
If we're being honest

She was a master projector
A bully and a pick-me
We'd be laid up every night, but
She couldn't stand me
'Collected rent money off me
Probably laughed to all her little friends
Real, real toxic
Like real, real toxic
We lived in perpetual hell
Some call it downtown LA

Getting the fuck on has been one of my biggest
    blessings
'Can't believe I was the last to know

She truly fucking hated me

Ten Toes

Don't you ever doubt, or
Underestimate my abilities
To be oh-so off you
'Cause I'll do it better

If you hang me out to dry, like
Washed clothes on a line
Stand ten toes on it

You won't find me upon your return
Because you will
They all do–and
I'll be long, long, gone

Shut me out if you want to
Just know your choice is permanent
Do me wrong–and
I'll never forget it

Don't you *ever* doubt, or
Underestimate my abilities
To be oh-so off you
'Cause I'll do it better

If you hang me out to dry
Stand ten toes on it

It's Time

Don't you think it's time that we
Stop pretending we don't need each other
I miss me before you left
I miss you before you started treating me as
Less-than

It's over?
No luxury of closure, hunh?
It's like, I mean, can we start all over again?

'Wanna be with you in new ways
Unrealistic
High time that I move on
In the same breath I can say
That I really wish we could start all over again, and
Go back to the magical high of our beginning
Before you started trippin' out on me
I'd love to feel your touch again
As only you can, and
Hear the sound of your voice
See the faint gap in your smile
Be in your arms or you in mine
Hang there for awhile

I miss you baby
Feel like I'm going insane
Who's holding you tonight?
Who will be for me?
What am I to do?

Quit playing
It's over?
No luxury of closure, hunh?
It's like, I mean, can we start all over again?
And no, not as friends
Don't even play in my face like that
No one loves you more than I do and you know
    it, too

Crying At The Orchestra

Strings glide
Sections riff harmoniously
Double bass in my gut
Cello in my heart

The conductor works to
Evoke tears out of me
Killing me softly

I'm crying at the orchestra, with
Damp, satin, beaded gloves, and
My pinky toe hurts
My shoes are too snug
In an attempt to be fancy, but
I'm not high brow

All these wordless melodies
Hurt more than they should
I can feel everything

You're the conductor
Evoking tears out of me
Killing me softly

All these wordless melodies
Hurt more than they should
I feel everything
I collect my program
Leave at the intermission

Sober

Damn, I really gotta feel *all* of this?
I really gotta let you see me in my natural state
Uninhibited by anything
Nothing to hide behind?
No added courage?
No curtain?
No veil?

Sober
With nowhere to run
Nowhere to go
All me?
Just me?

I suppose I really mean what I say
Is this off putting?
Am I too intense?
Should I lighten up?
Not really
Damn, I really gotta feel *all* of this

All But

I all but crashed out
I needn't run into the street
I hope I make it out alive
Got hella rage inside

All but lost my mind
Need all but a straight jacket
Hope I don't get cancer from all the anger kept
    beneath
And all the songs unsung
Eating my ass up from the inside

At least I can write poems
Release a little something
I all but quit my calling
I feel like–
This is a mistake
A big one
This is unfortunate
And unfun
This isn't good for me
Okay, maybe this is a crash out

Estranged

I won't bother you
You don't bother me
Tired of your half-assed text to fake wish me well
Your prayers from anywhere
What do you even believe?
Who are your prayers addressed to?
If your narrow mind
Is any indication
Yeah, don't pray for me

I get false truths
I get prying eyes
We're estranged and it never had to be this way
So
I won't bother you
You don't bother me

Leave me alone

Bed Of Our Own

What about the bed of our own?

What about the pillow talk in hushed tones?
What about me learning all of your body?
Your crown follicles to your toes

Sometimes they're painted white
Sometimes warm, butter yellow
Wait, are they clear these days?

Little purity
Little debauchery
We'll play it how you want it

There's an empty space
That I've been holding for you

I switch sides of the mattress just in case you have a
    preference
What about the bed of our own?

I'd conjure up strategies to elicit thumping
    jumps, and
Drizzling showers in between your thighs
Nothing is off limits in the bed of our own
Nothing is off limits for you
We'll play it how you want it

Do you have secrets?

Would you share them with me?
Or
You could tell me how your day was

There'd be a whole lotta
Cuddlin'
Fuckin'
Making love
Everything in the middle

I'd follow you in tight quarters of the mattress
So you don't go *nowhere*
So you don't get *too far from me*
I'd put you *through* the mattress
Play fight with pillows n' wrestle, I'd
Wrap my arm around you, and
Let it fall asleep just 'cause I don't want to move you
I'd
Watch you in wonder of how fucking beautiful you
    are to me, and
Gently snicker at your snores

There'd be a whole lotta love
Little debauchery
Little purity
We'll play it how you want it
In a bed of our own

Bone

You've got me on a
Pavlovian conditioning regimen
Give me a bone

Hate how I'm trained to
Leap to my phone with hopes of you
Scrolling down my story views

Just a—
Hoping that it's you
Hoping that it's you again
Hoping that it's you
Do you see me?
Do you miss me, back?

I would lie at your feet like a dog
Jump on you like a puppy
Follow you around
Wag at your joining

Ring a bell for me
And I come a-runnin'
Got a little somethin' for me?
When can I eat?
Give me a bone

Out Of Order

I'm
Out of order
Don't work
What's wrong with me?
Out of order
Don't waste your time
Save your troubles

I'm a heap of hodge-podge in the garage
Junkiest of junk in a miscellaneous drawer
Buttons and needles in a navy tin canister
No cookies

I'm all
Out of order
I'm false advertising
Better as a concept
Wonders in theory

I'm all
Out of order
Don't work
Out of order
Are you sure you want to love me?
Are you sure that you could love someone like me?

I'm a processed snack
Stuck in the vending machine
Please don't kick and pound

Jasmin Benward

I'm all
Out of order
Don't work
Out of order
I'm a clasp that don't grab nothing at the arcade
No prizes here
Save your coins

I'm all
Out of order
Don't work
Out of order

I'm the last bit of soap in a broken washing machine
No refunds
I'm a delayed traffic light when it should have turned
    green
Unknown muck beneath your shoe
Is this what you want to do?
Are you certain?
I'm imperfect
Neurodivergent
Perhaps a little *too* queer

I'm all
Out of order
Don't work
Out of order

Rust

You left me feeling exposed and ashamed of myself
Oxidized rust
Ring on the counter
Like I was the only one in the whole-wide-world
With a broken heart
No salt
No lemon
No vinegar
I don't dare get close to anyone else
Lest I be dazed and confused

It's your nature
All in what you do and how you move, with
No regard
No regard
No regard

I don't dare get close to anyone else
For fear of turning copper
Enduring steel wool

As Soon As

As soon as I get over you
Here you come with your bullshit
Making yourself known
Reminding me of all the things
Giving me hope

As soon as I get the courage, to
Delete the messages
Erase the pictures
Here you come with your nonsense
You ain't low

Were my astral messages on the backlog?
Is this another test to see if I mean what I say?
I believe you to be cruel
Don't give me a glimmer if there isn't one

I waited *so* long for a sign
I cried many a nights
I've tried to get a handle on me
I crashed out more than I could count

You know our bond's divine
Rare
Once in a lifetime
Despite being inopportune

You would have me believe that I was crazy and
    strung out

You would have me believe that we couldn't work
    it out
You would have me to believe
You would have me to
You would have me
You would have
You would–
You

As soon as I get the courage to move on
Here you go

Seasons Change

Angst, anger, awful all-knowing
Playing God
Silence as punishment
Use of the rod

An eerie distance
Telepathic tingles
Opposite ends east and west
The quiet breeds remembrance

I can't feel the warmth of last summer
Though I recall its heat
Yet, a winter's snow would have me forget
The life that we once lived

I make the effort to remedy
All the rain in LA
The snow in Atlanta
But I will not ask twice
I accept that seasons change

Warped Intimacy

I'm not unreasonable
If you didn't want me
You could have told me so
Instead of the bait and switch
Our love
A false victory
Filled with warped intimacy

You don't come home at night
'Jump straight into the shower
I recognize
I'm not your favorite person anymore
'Probably never was

At the party
No one knows I'm suffering
You hide distaste for me in plain sight, and
Lash out abundantly in private
I could scream
But I don't

Instead I take restorative approaches
Dreaming to love the cold out of you
The dinners
The walks
The talking
Meant nothing
Who were you thinking about across the table?
Who were you texting in the other room?

Jasmin Benward

Are they why you wrote me off?

My warmth is not enough for
Stone with coarse edges

How many nights did you watch me sleep hatefully?
Why send the flowers?
Why come to my show?
If you don't really support me

I'm not unreasonable
If you didn't want me
You could have told me so
Instead of the bait and switch
Our love
A false victory
Filled with warped intimacy

Cryptic Vinyl

A-side
Too late
You want her and not me
I'm too late
I was stuck in a loop
Full of patterns and body doubles
None of them were you
A never ending song
Encrypted messages in vinyl

B-side
I'm beside myself
I was stuck in a loop
'Couldn't get out
Finally made it, but
Not fast enough because
I couldn't get to you
I was stuck in a loop
And now you belong to someone else

Not A Writer

It's not wise to piss a writer off
We ramble on paper
We'll snitch anonymously
To get it off center
We'll call up them people
To edit the lines

We're getting street justice
A lick-back of sorts, with
Pen to the paper
Like a rapper getting in the booth
A diss track full of repetition, and
Iambic pentameter
Hate-speech in verse
Everybody's gonna know it
And you better had, too

It's not wise to piss a writer off
Failed connections turn to profit

To be mean to you at all
Would have meant that you were loved first, but
When the feelings go
So do the flowery, lofty words

Cool Off You

I bet that you can feel it now
I'm
Cool off you

I don't want it anymore
Tired of trying
Tired of chasing
Tired of making it right

One-sided fare *ain't it for me*
I've overstayed my welcome
I'm so cool off you

I kinda wanna be like you, though
I wish I could be cruel
I wish that I knew selfish
Just as well as you

You don't think for a second
How you impact me
You don't care that I was–
Begging
Hoping
Begging
Hoping
Pleading
Wondering

Jasmin Benward

You're full of shit
You're scum
You're a coward, for
Releasing the love within me
Big, golden retriever energy
And giving me black cat

Writer's Prey

What is there to even write about?
I'm not in love
Writing nonsense
Hoping for words
What is there to do when the muse is gone?
Huh!
Get another victim
Prey on someone else to feed the beast
Get off to get cracking on these WIPs

No one gives a shit that I've got deadlines
Where is the love?
Unrequited and otherwise?
Where are the toxic butterflies?
The coochie tingles?
Outrageous messages with invisible ink?
Where is the undeniable falsehood of promise?

I have not peered into longing eyes in awhile
I have not longed for anything or anyone
In a long, long time
I'm ejected from reality in some secret third space
Wondering in purgatory
Horny by the prospect of a best-seller's list

A Woman Knows

Liar, liar
A woman always knows

In the
Spiritual sense
There are
Accolades that you can't see
I bet you can feel me erasing you from my life
Just like I feel you pulling on me in my dreams
You ain't slick to a vessel of oil

I won't claim witch, but I'm gifted
You don't know?
It's telepathy
Don't deny it liar, liar
A woman always, always knows

You think I can't feel you stabbing me in my groin?
Where was this energy before?
I'd like to get a good night's rest
Without the help of supplements
I know it's you
A woman always, always knows

Ego is a killer
I don't want it anymore
I don't want you anymore
You complicate the easy

I bet you can feel me erasing you from my life
Just like I feel you pulling on me in my dreams
You ain't slick to a canister of Crisco

Palpitations

You sold me the dream, and
I bought it
No receipt, no refund
Well–I lost it
You did the most

You gave me itchy security blankets that didn't fold
I slept on the couch and floor
You give me heart palpitations
'Told you I'm invisibly disabled
Are you trying to kill me?
I bet you'd lie to my family
'Try to make it look like an accident

I've got a whole heart condition
You don't care to take it easy on me
You don't have to nudge, *I'll leave*
I don't wanna die here
And damn sure not with you

Banned

If I told you I didn't care that I was writing
A banned book
Would you believe me?
'Cause I don't give a fuck

Who are you?
Who do you think you are?
Who gave *you* permission?
You are *not* supreme to me

I know I occupy stolen lands
Why don't you?
I operate by invisible science
I am governed by sacred law
I have a voice, and
I have choices
I'll fuck who I want
And love who I want, too
My skin is a gift
Of course I'm feminist
Very pro-black–
The diaspora
The spectrum
The disability
The ghetto
The LGBTQIA+
Fucking all of it, every person
Prayers up to the Me Toos
Much love to the teachers and counselors

Jasmin Benward

Community lights and leads
Very free everybody, who needs liberation
Very land back
Kids' meals should be free
Don't get me started on food waste
What are we doing to the oceans?
Why is it snowing in Atlanta?
Like three times
Unhoused shouldn't be a concept
With all this fucking unused real estate
Like c'mon
This is a choice
This is deliberate choice

You know I don't give a fuck that I'm writing a
    banned book
'Hell, I'm just getting started

Stability

Hmm, how would stability
Look on me
I bet *real* nice

All the older women I know have fanciful-colored
    house robes
Hired help
And travel the globe

Would 'sholl be nice to have assistance come to *me*
Anyone to make my Black-disabledness smoother to
    swallow
Anyone to bring some ease

Someone to wash my car
Pluck tablescapes straight from my garden
Someone with good hands to tend to my head
Streams of income every which-a-way
Ooh, yeah
Hmm, stability

Who I gotta be?
And
What I gotta do?

All the older women I know have fanciful-colored
    tile in they crib
Brick and stone
Art from every nation

Jasmin Benward

Home libraries
Multiple rooms

They natural
Natural
Own their cells and very well

They call the shots
They tell *you* what to do
They alone
Or got a little friend
Mmm Hmm
And if they got a man he knows his place
Stays out the way
Ya feel me?
They foot-loose and foolery free!

'Cause I can see it for me, too
I should probably start investing
Decide on life's work
Ain't no retiring
I hear you'll rot and die
Best you keep your mind sharp
And stay busy
Definitely move those bag of bones
And often

The older women I know
They natural
Natural
Own their cells and very well

All the older women I know step out for the good
   shows
Orchestras and broadway
Have dinner after

All the older women I know *put that shit on*
Wear chunky jade-tone jewelry
And know their shade of red
Kiss you on both cheeks
'Got it going on
All 'cause they've worked for it

They natural
Natural
Own their cells and very well

Who I gotta be?
And
What I gotta do?

Hmm, how would stability
Look on me
I bet *real* nice!

Cross Country

Well, it's a damn good thing
That my reasoning
For LA
Wasn't *you*

I'm well lucky my dreams tell me what to do
If it were up to you I'd be anywhere
In some pit or begging on the street somewhere
Missing you
But I don't
And I thank God for it
My shit literally blew up
The moment I walked away

Can't Stand You

You're a bite to the inner lining of my cheek
Bleeding gums after flossing
You irk me
Such an inconvenience

You're a run in my hose when I needed coverage
    the most
A gnat up my nose
Such an–*ugh!*

You're excruciating hot-heat in the summer
You're a cherry-blueberry-slurpee brain freeze
Such an inconvenience

You're a bee sting under my pit
You're a fly on my freshly-made cookout plate
Hovering over my mac n'cheese
Soaking in my baked beans
Such a little shit

You're a step to the back of my heels
Work flats that don't fit
A blistering bump for constant contact
Just-a-flapping-and-a-rubbing me in all the
    wrong ways
You're a splinter in my index finger with no tweezers
Such an inconvenience
And no, I can't stand you

Crying In LA

Inevitable
I haven't changed
Always music
Always literature
Storytelling of sorts
Expression and telling my business
One prize
One honorarium at a time

Maybe I'll get an advance some day
'Get my shit adapted
Sit in a director's chair, and
Rub my chin away
I'd sure like to see my shit revised in yellow, golden-
 rod, and all the other colors

Is it not inevitable?
Am I not still fighting?
My manuscript is pulled up
In a side-by-side screen now
Am I not *that one?*
Am I not *that girl?*
Am I not *chosen?*
Is this not *already written?*

I praise the moment that
Happy tears, are
What have me crying in LA